LE CORDON BLEU

HOME COLLECTION

·DESSERTS·

MURDOCH BOOKS®
Sydney • London • Vancouver • New York

contents

recipe ratings ✸ *easy* ✸✸ *a little more care needed* ✸✸✸ *more care needed*

American apple pie

When pilgrims first settled in North America, they took with them apple seeds and a love of pies, sowing a national love affair with this cherished homely dessert. Cooking apples yield the best results.

*Preparation time **1 hour***
*Total cooking time **1 hour***
*Serves **4–6***

PASTRY
325 g (10¹/2 oz) plain flour
180 g (5³/4 oz) unsalted butter, cubed
2 tablespoons caster sugar

FILLING
800 g (1 lb 10 oz) large green apples
125 g (4 oz) sugar, and extra for sprinkling
1 teaspoon ground cinnamon
¹/4 teaspoon ground nutmeg
2¹/2 tablespoons plain flour
20 ml (³/4 fl oz) lemon juice
40 g (1¹/4 oz) unsalted butter, cubed

1 ` Preheat the oven to moderate 180°C (350°F/Gas 4). To make the pastry, work together the flour, butter, sugar and a pinch of salt in a food processor until the mixture resembles fine breadcrumbs. With the motor running, add 30 ml (1 fl oz) water and process until the mixture just comes together. Remove the dough, divide in half and form each portion into a thick disc. Cover with plastic wrap and chill for 15–20 minutes.

2 To make the filling, peel, quarter and core the apples, then slice thinly and place in a large bowl. Combine the sugar, cinnamon, nutmeg, flour and a good pinch of salt, and sprinkle the mixture over the apple. Add the lemon juice and toss well.

3 On a lightly floured surface, roll out a pastry portion 2.5 mm (¹/8 inch) thick, and 5 cm (2 inches) wider than a greased, shallow pie tin, 23 cm (9 inches) across the base. Carefully roll the dough onto a rolling pin, or fold into quarters, then ease into the tin. With your fingertips, press the dough into the tin to remove any air bubbles. Trim the excess pastry, leaving a 2.5 cm (1 inch) border of dough overhanging the edge of the tin.

4 Add the filling, then brush the pastry edges with water. Roll the remaining dough to the same thickness as before. Dot the apple with butter, place the dough on top and cut four steam holes. Trim the excess pastry, leaving a 1 cm (¹/2 inch) overhang, then press the edges together to seal them. Crimp the edges by pinching the pastry between thumb and forefinger into a zigzag design. Brush the top with water and sprinkle with extra sugar, then bake for 55–60 minutes. Cool the pie on a rack, and serve warm or cold.

Crème brûlée

The literal translation of this rich dessert is 'burnt cream'. Just before serving, chilled custard is sprinkled with sugar, which is quickly caramelised under a grill to form a brittle topping, creating a delicious contrast in flavour and texture to the smooth, creamy custard beneath.

*Preparation time **20 minutes + overnight refrigeration***
*Total cooking time **55 minutes***
Serves 6

4 egg yolks
2 1/2 tablespoons caster sugar
300 ml (10 fl oz) thick (double) cream
300 ml (10 fl oz) cream
vanilla extract or essence
3 tablespoons sugar

1 Preheat the oven to slow 150°C (300°F/Gas 2). Have six 100 ml (3 1/4 fl oz) capacity ramekins ready.

2 Whisk the egg yolks and sugar in a large heatproof bowl. Set aside. Bring all the cream and a few drops of vanilla to the boil in a heavy-based pan, then reduce the heat and simmer for about 8 minutes. Remove the pan from the heat and slowly pour the cream onto the egg mixture, whisking vigorously so the eggs do not scramble. Strain the custard into a large jug, then pour into the ramekins.

3 Place the ramekins in a baking dish. Pour enough hot water into the dish to reach 1 cm (1/2 inch) below the ramekin rims. Bake the custard for 40–45 minutes, or until just firm to the touch. Remove from the oven, allow to cool, then cover and refrigerate overnight.

4 To make the caramel, evenly sprinkle some sugar over the top of each custard using a teaspoon. Without piercing the skin of the custard, spread the sugar out very gently using a finger or the spoon, then repeat to form a second layer of sugar. Remove any sugar from the inside edges of the ramekins as it will burn on the dish. Place the ramekins on a metal tray and glaze under a very hot grill for 2–3 minutes, or until the sugar has melted and is just beginning to give off a haze. Allow the glaze to set or harden before serving.

Chef's tips This wonderful dessert is enhanced by fruit. Before pouring the custard into the ramekins, arrange a few berries (strawberries or raspberries are ideal) in the bottom of the dish, or prunes presoaked in Armagnac.

For best results, use a blowtorch to brown the sugar on top of the custards.

Hot Cointreau and orange soufflé

A beautifully risen, hot soufflé is always a sight to behold. This spectacular dessert, flavoured simply with the sweetness of sun-drenched orange, will create a sensation among even the most discerning dinner guests.

Preparation time **35 minutes**
Total cooking time **20 minutes**
Serves **6**

softened butter, for greasing
110 g (3³/4 oz) caster sugar, and extra for lining
2 tablespoons orange juice
2 teaspoons grated orange rind
1 tablespoon Cointreau
250 ml (8 fl oz) milk
¹/2 vanilla pod, split lengthways
4 eggs, separated
1 tablespoon plain flour
1 tablespoon cornflour
sifted icing sugar, to dust

1 Preheat the oven to moderate 180°C (350°F/Gas 4). Brush the insides of six 8 x 4 cm (3 x 1¹/2 inch) soufflé dishes with softened butter, working the brush from the bottom upwards. Refrigerate to set and repeat.

2 Half-fill a soufflé dish with some sugar, and without placing your fingers inside the dish, rotate it so that a layer of sugar adheres to the butter. Tap out the excess sugar and repeat with the remaining soufflé dishes.

3 Place the orange juice and grated rind in a small pan over medium-high heat. Simmer for 3–5 minutes to reduce the volume by three quarters—the mixture should be quite syrupy. Pour in the Cointreau, scraping the base of the pan with a wooden spoon. Remove from the heat and allow to cool.

4 Bring the milk and vanilla pod slowly to the boil. In a bowl, and using a wooden spoon, mix together 75 g (2¹/2 oz) of the caster sugar and two of the egg yolks, then mix in the flour and cornflour. Remove the vanilla pod from the boiling milk; stir a little of the milk into the egg mixture, then add all the mixture to the milk in the pan. Beat rapidly with the wooden spoon over medium heat until the mixture thickens and comes to the boil. Boil gently for 1 minute to cook the flour, stirring continuously to prevent sticking.

5 Pour the mixture into a clean bowl, stir to cool it slightly, then beat in the reduced orange sauce. Stir in the remaining two egg yolks and run a small piece of butter over the surface to melt and prevent a skin forming. (If you prefer, place a sheet of baking paper on the surface instead.)

6 In a clean, dry bowl, whisk the egg whites until they form soft peaks. Add the remaining sugar and whisk for 30 seconds. Add a third of the egg whites to the milk mixture and lightly beat in until just combined. Using a large metal spoon, fold in the remaining egg whites gently but quickly. Do not overmix, as this will cause the mixture to lose volume and become heavy.

7 Set the soufflé dishes on a baking tray. Spoon in the mixture to completely fill each dish, smooth the surface of each soufflé and sprinkle with sifted icing sugar. Roll your thumb around the inside of each mould to create a ridge that will enable the soufflé to rise evenly (see Chef's techniques, page 63). Bake for 12 minutes, or until well risen with a light crust. The soufflés should feel just set when pressed lightly with a fingertip. Serve at once.

Chef's tip This soufflé—to the end of step 4—can be prepared a few hours in advance.

Fruit terrine

This luscious dessert yields a truly fruit-filled flavour with every tingling mouthful.
The secret is to use two loaf tins instead of one, sitting one on top of the other to
prevent the fruit floating to the top before the jelly has set.

*Preparation time **40 minutes + 1–2 nights refrigeration***
*Total cooking time **5–10 minutes***
Serves 8

100 g (3¼ oz) blackcurrants
120 g (4 oz) redcurrants
110 g (3¾ oz) blueberries
350 g (11¼ oz) strawberries
225 g (7¼ oz) raspberries
4 leaves gelatine or 2 teaspoons gelatine powder
250 ml (8 fl oz) rosé wine
2 tablespoons caster sugar
1 tablespoon lemon juice
75 ml (2½ fl oz) sieved raspberry purée
  (see Chef's tips)

1 Sort through all the fruit and remove any stalks, then gently mix the fruit together, taking care not to bruise or damage any. Soak the gelatine leaves or powder, following the Chef's techniques on page 63.

2 Carefully arrange the fruit into a 1 kg (2 lb) loaf tin measuring 13 x 23 x 7 cm (5 x 9 x 2¾ inches), placing the smaller fruits on the bottom.

3 In a small pan, heat half the wine until it begins to simmer. Remove the pan from the heat and add the sugar, gelatine and lemon juice. Stir to dissolve. Add the remaining wine and the raspberry purée. Reserve 150 ml (5 fl oz) of the liquid and pour the rest over the fruit. Cover with plastic wrap. Place a lightly weighted 1 kg (2 lb) loaf tin on top, then refrigerate for at least 1 hour, or overnight if possible, until the terrine has set. Remove the top loaf tin and plastic wrap.

4 Gently warm the reserved wine-liquid and pour over the surface of the terrine. Cover again with plastic wrap and refrigerate overnight to set.

5 Just before serving, turn out the terrine by dipping the base of the tin very briefly in hot water and inverting it onto a plate. Slice the terrine, decorate with some extra fresh berries, and serve with crème fraîche.

Chef's tips Sieving 150 g (5 oz) of raspberries will produce the required quantity of raspberry purée.

Do not rinse the raspberries, and only rinse the other fruit if it is sandy.

Small strawberries give the best results in this fruit terrine, but if they are not available, you could use larger strawberries, cut in half.

Pink grapefruit sorbet

This sublime sorbet may be served in a tall glass as a refreshing dessert, or in a sherry glass as a palate cleanser. For best results, use an ice-cream churn.

*Preparation time **30 minutes + churning or beating + freezing***
*Total cooking time **1 minute***
*Serves **6***

175 g (5³/4 oz) caster sugar
200 ml (6¹/2 fl oz) pink or yellow grapefruit juice
   (about 3 grapefruit)
80 ml (2³/4 fl oz) lemon juice
250 ml (8 fl oz) dry white wine
75 ml (2¹/2 fl oz) Campari
6 sprigs of lemon balm or mint, to garnish

1   Stir the sugar and 175 ml (5³/4 fl oz) water in a small pan over low heat until the sugar dissolves. Bring to the boil, and allow to boil for 1 minute. Remove from the heat and leave to cool.

2   Combine the grapefruit and lemon juice and strain into a jug. Add the wine, Campari and cooled syrup.

3   Churn in an ice-cream maker for 30–40 minutes, or until thick and slushy, then transfer to a stainless steel container. Cover well with plastic wrap, then foil, and freeze for 1 hour before use.

4   Alternatively, freeze the mixture in a stainless steel container for about 3 hours, or until firm. Scoop into a large bowl and beat with an electric beater for 1–2 minutes, or until thick and creamy. Return the mixture to the container and freeze for 3 hours. Repeat the beating and freezing twice, then freeze overnight.

5   Remove from the freezer and refrigerate for about 20 minutes before serving. Scoop the mixture into well-chilled glasses and decorate each with a sprig of lemon balm or mint.

Chef's tip This sorbet can be frozen for up to 3 months.

Twice-baked chocolate cakes

These dark, fudgy cakes are sinfully rich and totally irresistible, with a dense base and a soufflé-like top that rises beautifully with the help of a paper collar. Sheer indulgence!

*Preparation time **1 hour 25 minutes***
*Total cooking time **35 minutes***
Serves 6

180 g (5³/4 oz) dark chocolate
150 g (5 oz) unsalted butter
3 tablespoons cocoa powder
6 eggs, separated
120 g (4 oz) caster sugar
cocoa and icing sugar, to dust

1 Preheat the oven to warm 170°C (325°F/Gas 3). Lightly grease six baking rings, each 7–8 cm (3 inches) across and 2 cm (³/4 inch) tall. (You can use 12 egg rings instead, stacking them two-high to form six 'rings'.) Line a baking tray with baking paper, grease the paper and set the baking rings on the tray.
2 Cut six strips of baking paper, each one 30 x 11 cm (12 x 4¹/2 inches) long. Make a 1 cm (¹/2 inch) fold along one long edge of each strip, then carefully make 1 cm (¹/2 inch) diagonal cuts into the fold, spaced about 5 mm (¹/4 inch) apart. Line the rings with the strips of paper so that the diagonal cuts sit very flat on the base of the tray. Press out any air bubbles with a pastry brush and refrigerate until ready to fill.

3 Melt the chocolate in a heatproof bowl set over a pan of simmering water. Add the butter and cocoa powder, whisk until smooth, and set aside.
4 Whisk the egg whites in a clean, dry bowl until stiff peaks form, then gradually beat in half the sugar until smooth and glossy. In a separate bowl, beat together the egg yolks and the remaining caster sugar for 5 minutes, or until light in colour and a ribbon forms when the whisk is lifted out of the bowl. Gently fold in the egg whites using a rubber spatula or large metal spoon. Gently fold in the chocolate mixture.
5 Divide half the mixture evenly between the rings, being careful not to get batter on the paper above. Bake for 15 minutes, then remove and cool completely. (The cakes will collapse and flatten.) Spoon the remaining mixture into each ring, covering the cake. Bake for 15–20 minutes. When cooked, the centre of the top of the cakes will stay steady when the tray is gently jiggled.
6 Slide a thin metal spatula under each ring and carefully loosen the cakes from the baking tray. Remove the rings, carefully peel the paper sleeves from the cakes and place on a serving plate. Dust with a little combined cocoa and icing sugar and serve at once.

Chef's tip Filling the rings with cake mixture is most easily done using a piping bag fitted with a medium tip.

Thin apple tart

This spectacular tart—Tarte fine aux pommes—has a crisp shortcrust base spread with almond cream and topped with glazed apples. This recipe calls for Golden Delicious apples, but whichever variety you use, recall the ancient wisdom of Horace: the best apples of all are those picked by the light of a waning moon!

*Preparation time **1 hour + 40 minutes refrigeration***
*Total cooking time **1 hour***
*Serves **6–8***

SHORTCRUST PASTRY
100 g (3¹/4 oz) plain flour
50 g (1³/4 oz) icing sugar
50 g (1³/4 oz) unsalted butter
I egg yolk
vanilla extract or essence

ALMOND CREAM
3 tablespoons icing sugar
30 g (I oz) unsalted butter, softened
I teaspoon vanilla extract or essence
I egg yolk
3 tablespoons ground almonds

500 g (I lb) Golden Delicious apples, or similar variety
juice of I lemon
apricot jam, for glazing

1 To make the pastry, sift the flour and icing sugar into a bowl, then rub in the butter until the mixture resembles breadcrumbs. Make a well in the centre and add the egg yolk, a few drops of vanilla, a pinch of salt and enough cold water to help form a dough. Turn out onto a floured surface and gather the dough together to make a smooth ball. Cover with plastic wrap and refrigerate for 30 minutes, or until just firm.
2 Preheat the oven to moderate 180°C (350°F/Gas 4). Remove the plastic wrap from the chilled pastry, then very gently roll out the pastry between two sheets of greaseproof or baking paper to a thickness of 2.5 mm (1/8 inch). Carefully ease the pastry into a greased, shallow loose-bottomed flan tin, 22 cm (8³/4 inches) across the base.
3 Blind bake the pastry for 20 minutes, following the Chef's techniques on page 62. Remove the rice or baking beans and baking paper, then bake for a further 10 minutes, covering the pastry with foil if the pastry looks as though it might burn. Remove from the oven and allow to cool.
4 To make the almond cream, beat together the icing sugar, butter and vanilla until light and creamy. Add the egg yolk and beat well, then add the ground almonds. Spread the mixture in an even layer over the cooled pastry shell.
5 Peel, quarter and core the apples, then sprinkle them with lemon juice. Thinly slice the apples and arrange in overlapping circles over the layer of almond cream. Bake for 20–25 minutes, or until the apples are cooked. Set on a wire rack to cool.
6 When the tart has cooled, place some apricot jam in a small pan and bring to the boil. (Add a spoonful of water if the jam becomes too thick for spreading.) Sieve the jam and, using a pastry brush, lightly dab the surface of the tart with the jam—this will give the apples a nice shine and prevent them drying out.

Chef's tips Handle the pastry as little as possible, and work quickly and lightly.

Make sure the tart has cooled before brushing it with jam. If the tart is still hot, the fruit will simply soak up the jam and the tart will lose its shine when it cools.

Vanilla ice cream

*No commercial ice cream can ever compare with the creamy, decadent
richness of the home-made variety. This classic favourite is peppered with fine black specks:
the tiny seeds of the vanilla pod, which release a fabulous flavour. For a light, smooth
result every time, with minimal fuss, an ice-cream churn is highly recommended.*

*Preparation time **20 minutes + churning or beating
   + freezing***
*Total cooking time **10 minutes***
Serves 4

5 egg yolks
100 g (3¼ oz) caster sugar
375 ml (12 fl oz) milk
1 vanilla pod, split lengthways
125 ml (4 fl oz) thick (double) cream

1 Whisk the egg yolks and sugar in a heatproof bowl
until thick and creamy and almost white. Bring the milk
and vanilla pod slowly to the boil in a heavy-based
pan. Gradually whisk the boiling milk into the eggs and
sugar, then transfer the mixture to a clean pan. Stir
constantly with a wooden spoon over low heat for
about 3–5 minutes, or until the custard thickly coats the
back of the spoon. Ensure that the mixture does not
boil, as this will cause it to separate.

2 Pour through a fine strainer into a clean bowl. Place
the bowl in some iced water to cool. When the custard
is very cold, stir in the cream, then pour the mixture
into an ice-cream churn and churn for 10–20 minutes,
or until the paddle leaves a trail in the ice cream, or the
ice cream holds its own shape. Remove from the churn
and freeze in an airtight, stainless steel container for
3–4 hours or overnight.

3 Alternatively, freeze the custard and cream mixture
in a 1 litre container for 3 hours, or until firm. Scoop
into a large bowl and beat with an electric beater for
1–2 minutes, or until thick and creamy. Return the
mixture to the container and freeze for 3 hours. Repeat
the beating and freezing twice, then freeze overnight.

Chef's tip This ice cream can take on a range of flavours.
A little coffee extract may be added to the custard at
the end of step 1, or 50–100 g (1¾–3¼ oz) chopped
chocolate may be added to the milk before boiling.
Another delicious option is to fold amaretto or crushed
biscuits into the frozen ice cream before it is stored.

Thin shortbreads with fresh cream and fruit

This easy-to-assemble dessert is a wicked union of sweet red fruit and luscious whipped cream, anchored in rounds of lemon-tinged shortbread.

*Preparation time **45 minutes + refrigeration***
*Total cooking time **20–25 minutes***
Serves 4–6

SHORTBREAD PASTRY
300 g (10 oz) unsalted butter, softened
150 g (5 oz) icing sugar
finely grated rind of 1 lemon
vanilla extract or essence
1 egg, lightly beaten
450 g (14¼ oz) plain flour, sifted

FILLING
200 ml (6½ fl oz) thick (double) cream
1 teaspoon vanilla extract or essence
caster sugar, to taste
400 g (12¾ oz) assorted red fruits, such as
  strawberries, raspberries and redcurrants

40 g (1¼ oz) icing sugar, for dusting
fresh mint leaves, to garnish

1 Brush two baking trays with melted butter and refrigerate. Preheat the oven to warm 160°C (315°F/ Gas 2–3). To make the pastry, cream the butter and sugar until pale and smooth. Stir in the rind and a few drops of vanilla. Add the egg gradually, beating well after each addition. Add the flour in one batch and stir until combined: the mixture will be very soft and sticky.

2 Divide the mixture in two. Roll out each portion 2.5 mm (1/8 inch) thick between two layers of well-floured greaseproof or baking paper, working quickly and lightly. Place on the chilled trays with the paper still attached, then refrigerate until firm.

3 Slide the pastry off the trays onto a work surface. Remove the top piece of paper, dip an 8.5 cm (3½ inch) fluted pastry-cutter in flour and cut three discs per serve. Ease the discs off the bottom sheet of paper onto the buttered baking trays and prick with a fork. Bake for 20–25 minutes, or until golden; allow to cool briefly before removing from the tray to cool on a rack.

4 To make the filling, pour the cream into a bowl, add the vanilla, and sugar to taste. Whisk into soft peaks. (Do not overwhisk as the cream will overthicken and split.) Spoon into a piping bag fitted with an 8-cut star nozzle.

5 To assemble, pipe some cream onto the middle of a disc; arrange some fruit around the cream (but not over the edge). Top with a disc, repeat the fruit and cream, then top with a third disc, dusted with icing sugar. Finish the remaining rounds, reserving some fruit. Transfer to serving plates and decorate with mint and reserved fruit.

Chocolate and Cointreau mousse

Mousse in French literally means froth or foam. This melt-in-the-mouth mousse marries the classic flavours of chocolate and orange, is simple to prepare, and makes a magical finale to any meal.

*Preparation time **40 minutes + 1 hour refrigeration***
*Total cooking time **5 minutes***
Serves 4–6

125 g (4 oz) dark chocolate
50 g (1 3/4 oz) unsalted butter
70 ml (2 1/4 fl oz) orange juice
2 1/2 tablespoons cocoa powder
2 eggs, separated
25 ml (3/4 fl oz) Cointreau
100 ml (3 1/4 fl oz) cream, for whipping
1 egg white, extra
1 1/2 tablespoons caster sugar
orange segments and whipped cream, to serve

1 Place the chocolate, butter and orange juice in a heatproof bowl over a pan of just-simmering water. When the chocolate and butter have melted, stir in the cocoa powder. Remove from the heat and whisk in the egg yolks and Cointreau. Leave to cool.
2 In a chilled bowl, beat the cream until soft peaks form. Cover and refrigerate until ready to use.
3 Beat all the egg whites in a clean, dry bowl until soft peaks form. Add the sugar; beat until smooth and glossy.
4 Using a large metal spoon, gently fold the egg whites into the cooled chocolate mixture. Before they are completely incorporated, fold in the whipped cream. Transfer the mixture into individual serving dishes or a large serving bowl and refrigerate for at least 1 hour. Serve with orange segments and whipped cream.

Bread and butter pudding with panettone

When the yearning strikes for a homely dessert, bread and butter pudding is hard to beat.
For special occasions, this humble and economical dish can be transformed into something really
marvellous with glacé fruits, a dash of rum, some brioche or, as in this case, Italian panettone.

*Preparation time **20 minutes***
*Total cooking time **50 minutes***
Serves 4

3 tablespoons sultanas
2 tablespoons rum, brandy or amaretto
250 g (8 oz) panettone
3 eggs
3 tablespoons caster sugar
500 ml (16 fl oz) milk
1 vanilla pod, split lengthways
1 tablespoon apricot jam, warmed
icing sugar, to dust

1 Preheat the oven to warm 160°C (315°F/Gas 2–3). Place the sultanas in a 23 cm (9 inch) oval pie dish and pour the alcohol over the top.
2 Cut the panettone to make two or three round slices about 1 cm (1/2 inch) thick, then remove the crust. Cut each slice into four quarters (almost triangles). Neatly overlap them in the base of the pie dish.
3 Whisk the eggs and sugar in a heatproof bowl until just combined. Place the milk and vanilla pod in a pan, bring to the boil, then slowly pour the scalding milk into the egg and sugar mixture, whisking continuously.
4 Pour the mixture through a fine strainer into the pie dish, over the panettone. Place the pie dish in a baking tray half full of hot water. Cook for 40–45 minutes, or until the custard has set and is golden brown.
5 Remove the pie dish from the oven and, while the pudding is still warm, brush the surface with the warm apricot jam. Sprinkle with icing sugar and serve either hot or cold.

Chef's tips If the panettone is not a sweet one, simply increase the sugar to taste.

Fruit loaf is a perfect alternative to panettone as it already has a loaf shape. Simply cut off the crusts, slice the bread and cut each slice in half to form triangles.

Spiced poached pears with orange butter

In this simply elegant dessert, the pears are gently infused with the flavours of real vanilla and star anise, then fringed with wisps of candied peel, and served with a Cointreau-laced orange sauce.

Preparation time **1 hour**
Total cooking time **1 hour**
Serves 4

1 lemon
800 g (1 lb 10 oz) oranges
660 g (1 lb 6 oz) sugar
1 vanilla pod, split lengthways
3 sticks cinnamon
10 whole black peppercorns
4 star anise
3 cloves
pinch of nutmeg
6 pears, about 1.5 kg (3 lb)
fresh mint leaves, to garnish

ORANGE BUTTER
400 ml (12³/4 fl oz) orange juice
120 g (4 oz) unsalted butter, cut into cubes
2 tablespoons Cointreau

1 Peel the rind off the lemon and an orange with a vegetable peeler, without scraping the bitter white pith. Place the rind in a large pan with 2 litres water and 500 g (1 lb) of the sugar. Wrap the whole spices in muslin for easy removal later, and add them to the pan with the nutmeg. Stir over a low heat until the sugar has dissolved, then bring to a gentle simmer.

2 Peel the pears, leaving the stems intact, and add them to the simmering liquid. Allow them to simmer gently for 20 minutes, or until easily pierced with a knife tip. They should be just tender, but not soft. Remove from the heat and allow to cool in the liquid.

3 To make the orange butter, bring the orange juice to the boil in a small pan, then reduce the heat and simmer for 30 minutes, or until reduced by three quarters. Remove from the heat and whisk in the butter, a few pieces at a time. Whisk in the Cointreau and set aside.

4 Peel the rind from the remaining oranges, avoiding the bitter white pith. Cut the rind into thin strips and set aside. Cut the tops and bottoms off the oranges and discard. Place the oranges on a cutting board and with a sharp knife, cut from top to bottom, following the curve of the fruit to expose the flesh. Cut between the membranes to remove the orange segments. Set aside.

5 Place the strips of orange rind in a small pan and cover with water. Bring to the boil, strain the rind and rinse with cold water. Return to the pan with 160 ml (2³/4 fl oz) water and the remaining sugar. Stir over low heat to dissolve the sugar, then bring to the boil. Reduce the heat and leave the rinds to slowly candy in the syrup for 20 minutes—they will become translucent. Strain over a bowl, reserving the liquid. Add the liquid to the orange butter, and cool the rinds on a piece of baking paper.

6 Remove two of the cooled pears and cut them in half. Remove the cores and stems, then slice the pear halves thinly. Place a sliced half on each plate, as well as a whole pear. Drizzle the orange butter around and arrange some candied rind on top of the pear slices. Decorate with the orange segments and fresh mint.

Chef's tip Poached pears will improve in flavour and texture if prepared 1 or 2 days in advance. They can be refrigerated for up to 1 week in the syrup. For extra colour, add 2 tablespoons of grenadine syrup to the sugar mixture when candying the orange rind.

Hot passion fruit soufflés

Feather-light, these wonderful soufflés tantalise the tastebuds with the
tart sweetness and tropical perfume of passion fruit.

Preparation time 20 minutes
Total cooking time 20 minutes
Serves 4

softened unsalted butter, for greasing
120 g (4 oz) caster sugar, and extra for coating
12 passion fruit or 120 g (4 oz) passion fruit pulp
6 egg whites
icing sugar, for dusting

1 Prepare four 10 cm (4 inch) 250 ml (8 fl oz) capacity ramekins or individual soufflé moulds by brushing the inside of each with softened butter, using a pastry brush. Refrigerate the moulds until the butter is firm, then brush on another layer of butter and chill again. Half-fill one of the moulds with the extra sugar, and without placing your fingers inside the mould, rotate it so that a layer of sugar adheres to the butter. Tap out the excess sugar and use it to coat the other moulds.

2 Preheat the oven to warm 160°C (315°F/Gas 2–3). Pass the passion fruit pulp through a sieve into a bowl and add 60 g (2 oz) sugar. Discard the seeds.

3 Whisk the egg whites until soft peaks form. Sprinkle the remaining sugar onto the egg whites and whisk for 1 minute. Gently fold the egg whites into the passion fruit pulp. Spoon a quarter of the mixture into each mould and smooth the surface. Sprinkle the top of each soufflé with sifted icing sugar, then run your thumb around the inside of the mould to create a ridge to help the soufflé rise evenly (see Chef's techniques, page 63).

4 Place the moulds in a baking tray or large ovenproof dish, and pour in enough hot water to reach halfway up the moulds. Bake for 20 minutes, or until well risen. Once cooked, remove from the oven, sprinkle with more sifted icing sugar and serve immediately.

Bavarian vanilla cream

A bavarois is an egg-based custard folded through with whipped cream, and flavoured with chocolate, coffee, praline or even fruit. This bavarois is simply laced with real vanilla.

*Preparation time **1 hour + 1 hour refrigeration***
*Total cooking time **10 minutes***
Serves 4

3 leaves gelatine or 1¹/₂ teaspoons gelatine powder
2 eggs, separated
3 tablespoons caster sugar
250 ml (8 fl oz) milk
1 vanilla pod, split lengthways
125 ml (4 fl oz) thick (double) cream, lightly whipped

1 Lightly grease four 250 ml (8 fl oz) capacity moulds of any shape, then soak the gelatine leaves or powder, following the Chef's techniques on page 63.
2 Beat the egg yolks and sugar in a bowl until thick, creamy and almost white. Slowly bring the milk and vanilla pod to the boil.
3 Follow the method for making custard in the Chef's techniques on page 63. Stir the soaked gelatine into the hot custard, ensuring the gelatine dissolves completely, strain into a clean bowl, then leave over a bowl of ice until almost at the point of setting, stirring occasionally, and checking often.
4 Whisk the egg whites until stiff—they should stand in shiny peaks when the whisk is lifted. Using a metal spoon, fold the lightly whipped cream into the cold custard, then carefully fold in the egg whites.
5 Spoon the mixture into the moulds and refrigerate for at least 1 hour, or until set. Unmould by gently shaking at an angle of 45°, or dipping the base of the mould briefly in boiling water and tapping onto a serving dish.

Chef's tips The egg whites should not be whisked too far in advance: standing will make the volume drop, and also result in a dry, granular texture. Adding a pinch of sugar while the egg whites are lightly foaming will stabilise them and help them whisk stiff more easily.

Ensure the custard is cold before adding the cream: if the cream melts, the dessert will lose volume.

Rhubarb and almond tart

This tart has a rich, moist filling and can be enjoyed on its own, or with crème anglaise or ice cream. It keeps well and can be made a few days in advance. Fresh plums, apricots or pears can be used instead of rhubarb.

Preparation time **1 hour + 40 minutes refrigeration**
Total cooking time **40 minutes**
Serves **6–8**

PASTRY
125 g (4 oz) unsalted butter, softened
3 tablespoons caster sugar
1 egg, beaten
200 g (6½ oz) plain flour

ALMOND CREAM
100 g (3¼ oz) unsalted butter, softened
100 g (3¼ oz) caster sugar
2 teaspoons finely grated lemon rind
2 eggs
100 g (3¼ oz) ground almonds
1 tablespoon plain flour

2 tablespoons raspberry jam
1 stick rhubarb, thinly sliced
2 tablespoons flaked almonds
2 tablespoons apricot jam
icing sugar, for dusting

1 To make the pastry, beat the butter and sugar in a bowl until well blended using a wooden spoon or electric beaters. Add the egg gradually, beating well after each addition. Sift in the flour and a pinch of salt and mix lightly using a flat-bladed knife until the mixture just comes together—do not overmix. Gather together to form a rough ball and place on a large piece of plastic wrap. Gently flatten to a 1 cm (½ inch) thickness, then wrap and refrigerate for 20 minutes.

2 To make the almond cream, beat the butter, sugar and lemon rind in a small bowl using a wooden spoon, whisk or electric beaters. Gradually beat in the eggs. Stir in the almonds and flour and set aside.

3 To assemble, roll out the pastry on a floured surface (or between two sheets of baking paper) 2.5 mm (1/8 inch) thick. Ease into a greased, loose-bottomed, fluted or plain flan tin, 20 cm (8 inches) across the base. Trim the edges, pierce the base lightly with a fork and spread with raspberry jam. Spread the almond cream over the top, just level with the pastry edge. Decorate with rhubarb, slightly pushing into the almond cream. Sprinkle with flaked almonds and chill for 20 minutes.

4 Preheat the oven to moderate 180°C (350°F/Gas 4). Place the tart on a baking tray and bake for 10 minutes to help set the pastry. Reduce the oven temperature to warm 160°C (315°F/Gas 2–3) and bake for a further 30–35 minutes, or until the almond filling is golden brown and springs back when lightly touched.

5 In a small pan, heat the apricot jam with 3 teaspoons water. When the mixture has melted and begins to boil, sieve it into a small bowl, and while still hot, brush it over the tart. Allow the jam to cool, then sift a light dusting of icing sugar across the top.

Chef's tips Handle the pastry as little as possible: work quickly and lightly. Always rest or chill pastry before rolling to make it easier to manage. Resting just before baking helps prevent shrinkage and loss of shape.

To make the pastry in a food processor, process the flour, butter and sugar into fine crumbs, add the egg and process in short bursts until the pastry just comes together. Tip onto a lightly floured work surface and draw the pastry together by hand.

Creamed rice pudding

Whipped cream makes this rice pudding extravagantly rich and creamy.
A sharp fruit sauce or compote is the perfect accompaniment.

*Preparation time **10 minutes***
*Total cooking time **30 minutes***
Serves 4–6

3 tablespoons short-grain rice
600 ml (20 fl oz) milk
1 vanilla pod, split lengthways
2 tablespoons caster sugar
150 ml (5 fl oz) cream, for whipping

1 Place the rice in a colander and rinse thoroughly under running water until the water runs clear. Drain.
2 Pour the milk into a medium heavy-based pan, add the vanilla pod and rice, then bring slowly to the boil.

Reduce the heat and gently simmer, stirring often, for about 30 minutes, or until the rice is soft and creamy. When a spoon is drawn across the base of the pan, a clear parting in the rice should be left behind.
3 Stir in the sugar and transfer the mixture to a large bowl. Remove the vanilla pod, cover the surface with plastic wrap and allow to cool. Lightly whip the cream in a separate bowl until soft peaks form. When the pudding is cold, carefully fold in the cream. Serve with a fruit sauce or compote.

Chef's tip Because this dessert is so rich, you may choose to add only half of the whipped cream. To vary the flavour, try adding a small pinch of cinnamon or nutmeg with the sugar.

Apple strudel

In Vienna it is said that in the making of a perfect apple strudel, the dough is stretched so finely that a love letter may be read through it.

Preparation time **40 minutes + 30 minutes resting**
Total cooking time **50 minutes**
Serves 6–8

185 g (6 oz) strong or plain flour
I egg, lightly beaten
120 g (4 oz) unsalted butter
90 g (3 oz) fresh breadcrumbs
3 tablespoons caster sugar
2 teaspoons ground cinnamon
600 g (1¼ lb) cooking or very sharp dessert apples
60 g (2 oz) sultanas
icing sugar, for dusting

1 Sift the flour and a pinch of salt into a large bowl. Make a well in the centre, add the beaten egg and 75 ml (2½ fl oz) warm water, and mix with your hands to a smooth dough. With the bowl tipped to one side, and with open fingers, beat the dough, rotating your wrist. The dough is ready when it pulls away from the bowl and is difficult to beat. Place in a clean, lightly floured bowl, cover and leave in a warm place for 15 minutes.

2 Melt half of the butter in a pan. Slowly fry the breadcrumbs until golden brown, then set aside to cool in a bowl. Mix the sugar and cinnamon in a small bowl. Preheat the oven to moderate 180°C (350°F/Gas 4).

3 Thoroughly flour one side of a large clean tea towel, place the pastry on top and, with your fingers, gently stretch the dough to a large rectangle about 50 x 60 cm (20 x 24 inches); cover with a tea towel and set aside for 15 minutes. Melt the remaining butter and set aside.

4 Peel, quarter, core and finely slice the apples, and combine with the breadcrumbs, cinnamon mixture and sultanas. Brush the dough liberally with the melted butter, then sprinkle the apple mixture all over the dough. Trim away the thick edge with a pair of scissors.

5 Pick up the tea towel from the shorter side, and push away and down from you to lightly roll the strudel up like a swiss roll. Tip the strudel carefully onto a tray, seam-side down or to one side. Leave the strudel straight, or curve it lightly into the traditional 'crescent'. Brush the pastry well with any remaining butter.

6 Bake for 35–45 minutes, or until crisp and golden. Cool slightly, sprinkle with icing sugar and serve warm with vanilla custard, ice cream or whipped cream.

Clafoutis

This classic dessert is based on a dish originating in the French country region of Limousin, where clafoutis is enjoyed when sweet, dark cherries are ripe. Cherries are the favoured fruit for this dessert, although plums or pears may also be used.

*Preparation time **40 minutes***
*Total cooking time **45 minutes***
Serves 4

1 fresh peach or 2 tinned peach halves, drained
  of syrup
250 g (8 oz) cherries
500 ml (16 fl oz) thick (double) cream
1 vanilla pod, split lengthways
6 egg yolks
1 egg
1 tablespoon custard powder
2¹/₂ tablespoons plain flour
25 ml (³/₄ fl oz) Cointreau
icing sugar, for dusting

1 Preheat the oven to slow 150°C (300°F/Gas 2). If you are using a fresh peach, plunge it in boiling water for 10–20 seconds, then transfer to a bowl of iced water. Peel the peach and cut around the fruit towards the stone. Gently twist the halves in opposite directions to expose the stone, then lift out the stone with a knife. If the peach is too slippery, simply cut the flesh from the stone. Process or sieve one peach half and measure out 50 ml (1³/4 fl oz) of purée. Slice the remaining peach half into neat segments and set aside. Pit the cherries and set aside.

2 Place the cream in a heavy-based pan with the vanilla pod, then heat until scalding—this is when bubbles form around the edge of the cream surface, yet the cream is not boiling. Remove the vanilla pod.

3 Whisk the egg yolks and the whole egg together in a large bowl. Beat in the custard powder and flour, then stir in the peach purée. Whisk the scalding cream into the egg mixture. Add the Cointreau and stir.

4 Lightly grease a 2 litre capacity shallow ovenproof dish with softened butter. Place all the fruit in the dish. Pour the custard over and bake for about 40 minutes, or until a skewer inserted into the centre of the dessert comes out clean. Immediately sift the icing sugar over the top. Serve hot.

Iced raspberry soufflé

*This chilled raspberry soufflé always looks wonderful and is a great
conversation piece. It can also be made days—if not weeks—ahead,
leaving more time for you to spend with your guests.*

Preparation time **45 minutes + 6 hours freezing
+ 30 minutes standing**
Total cooking time **10 minutes**
Serves **4–6**

550 g (1 lb 1³/4 oz) raspberries
250 g (8 oz) caster sugar
5 egg whites
400 ml (12³/4 fl oz) cream, for whipping
200 ml (6¹/2 fl oz) cream, for whipping, extra
fresh raspberries, to garnish
sprigs of fresh mint, to garnish

1 Purée the raspberries in a food processor, then press
through a fine sieve to eliminate the seeds. Weigh out
300 g (10 oz) of raspberry purée and set aside.
2 Cut out a piece of greaseproof or baking paper
to measure 25 x 9 cm (10 x 3¹/2 inches). Wrap the
paper around the outside of a 1 litre, 18 cm (7 inch)
soufflé dish to make a collar. Secure the overlapping

paper in place with tape or kitchen string, keeping the
paper free of creases.
3 Place the caster sugar and 60 ml (2 fl oz) water in a
medium heavy-based pan and heat gently to dissolve
the sugar. Bring the syrup to the boil, then follow the
Chef's techniques for making Italian meringue on
page 63.
4 In a separate bowl, whip the first quantity of cream
to soft peaks.
5 Using a metal spoon, gently fold the meringue into
the reserved raspberry purée until thoroughly mixed,
then fold in the cream until the streaks disappear. Be
careful not to overmix, as this will cause the cream to
thicken and separate and make the soufflé look grainy.
6 Spoon the mixture into the soufflé dish right up to
the edge of the paper collar, then gently smooth the
surface of the soufflé. Freeze for a minimum of 6 hours.
Just before serving, peel off the paper collar and allow
the soufflé to stand for 30 minutes to soften. Whip the
extra cream and use it to decorate the soufflé. Top with
the fresh raspberries and sprigs of mint.

Lemon meringue pie

This time-honoured favourite—a shortcrust pastry case smothered by a creamy lemon filling and a layer of meringue—is often served for Sunday lunch. It should be baked and served on the same day.

*Preparation time **45 minutes + 40 minutes refrigeration***
*Total cooking time **45 minutes***
Serves 6

SHORTCRUST PASTRY
200 g (6¹/2 oz) plain flour, sifted
I teaspoon caster sugar
100 g (3¹/4 oz) unsalted butter, chopped
I egg
I teaspoon vanilla extract or essence

LEMON FILLING
3 egg yolks
150 g (5 oz) caster sugar
2 teaspoons finely grated lemon rind
juice of 3 lemons
30 g (I oz) unsalted butter

200 g (6¹/2 oz) caster sugar
4 egg whites
I tablespoon icing sugar, for dusting

1 To make the shortcrust pastry, sieve the flour, sugar and a good pinch of salt into a bowl. Add the butter and rub between your fingertips until the mixture resembles fine breadcrumbs. Make a well in the centre. Combine the egg, vanilla and 2 teaspoons water and pour into the well. Slowly stir together with a flat-bladed knife, adding more flour if the mixture is slightly sticky. Gather the dough together in a ball, wrap in plastic wrap and refrigerate for 20 minutes.

2 Preheat the oven to moderate 180°C (350°F/Gas 4). Gently roll the pastry between two sheets of baking paper to about 2.5 mm (¹/8 inch) thick, then ease into a lightly greased, loose-bottomed fluted flan tin, 22 cm (8³/4 inches) across the base. Blind bake for 10 minutes, following the Chef's techniques on page 62. Remove the rice or baking beans and the paper. Bake for 10 more minutes, or until the centre begins to colour. Remove from the oven and cool on a wire rack.

3 To prepare the filling, heat a medium pan of water until gently simmering. Whisk or beat the egg yolks and sugar in a large heatproof bowl until light and creamy. Add the lemon rind, juice and then the butter. Sit the bowl over the pan of barely simmering water and whisk continuously for 15–20 minutes, or until thickened. When ready, the mixture will leave a 'ribbon' when drizzled from the whisk. While the filling is still hot, pour into the cool, prebaked flan case.

4 Place the sugar and 50 ml (1³/4 fl oz) water in a medium heavy-based pan and heat gently to dissolve the sugar. Bring to the boil, then follow the Chef's techniques for making Italian meringue on page 63.

5 Place the meringue in a piping bag fitted with a 1 cm (¹/2 inch) star nozzle. Starting in the centre, pipe the meringue in continuous concentric circles covering the entire flan, keeping the meringue inside the pastry edge. Dust the surface with icing sugar. Bake for 5 minutes, or until the meringue is lightly coloured. Leave to cool and then refrigerate for 20 minutes, or until the filling is set.

Chef's tip If possible, refrigerate the dough overnight. This helps prevent the pastry shrinking during cooking.

Crêpes Suzette

In this illustrious dessert, very fine pancakes are warmed in a lightly caramelised orange butter sauce, then doused with Cointreau and ignited to flaming glory, ending any repast on a note of unforgettable flourish.

Preparation time **30 minutes + 30 minutes resting**
Total cooking time **45 minutes**
Makes 12 crêpes

CREPE BATTER
90 g (3 oz) plain flour
1 teaspoon caster sugar
2 eggs, plus 1 egg yolk, lightly beaten
170 ml (5¹/₂ fl oz) milk
25 g (³/₄ oz) clarified butter, melted (see page 62)

clarified butter, for cooking (see page 62)

SAUCE
4 white sugar cubes
800 g (1 lb 10 oz) oranges
40 g (1¹/₄ oz) clarified butter, melted (see page 62)
3 tablespoons caster sugar
45 ml (1¹/₂ fl oz) Cointreau
30 ml (1 fl oz) brandy

1 To make the batter, sift the flour into a bowl with a pinch of salt and the sugar. Make a well in the centre, then add the eggs and extra egg yolk. Mix well with a wooden spoon or whisk, gradually incorporating the flour. Combine the milk with 60 ml (2 fl oz) water and gradually add to the batter. Add the clarified butter and beat until smooth. Cover and set aside for 30 minutes.
2 Melt a little clarified butter in a shallow heavy-based or non-stick pan measuring 15–17 cm (6–6³/4 inches) across the base. When a haze forms, pour off any surplus butter, leaving a fine coating sufficient to cook one crêpe. Tilt the pan and pour in a little batter, swirling to coat just the bottom of the pan with a thin layer. Cook for 1–2 minutes, or until the edges are lightly brown. Loosen the edges with a flat-bladed knife or spatula and turn or flip the crêpe over. Cook for about 1 minute, then turn onto a sheet of greaseproof or baking paper and cover with a tea towel. Repeat until all the batter has been used up, each time lightly coating the pan with clarified butter.
3 To make the sauce, rub all the sugar cube sides over the rind of an orange to soak up the oily zest, then crush the cubes with the back of a wooden spoon. Juice the oranges to produce 315 ml (10 fl oz) liquid. Over gentle heat, melt the clarified butter in a wide shallow pan or frying pan. Dissolve the crushed sugar in the butter, then add the caster sugar. Cook, stirring, for 2 minutes. Slowly add the orange juice, keeping well clear of the pan as the mixture may spit. Increase the heat to medium and simmer until reduced by one third.
4 Fold the crêpes in half, then into triangles. Place them in the orange sauce, slightly overlapping, with their points showing. Tilt the pan, scoop up the sauce and pour it over the crêpes to moisten them well.
5 Cook over low heat for 2 minutes. Turn off the heat and have a saucepan lid ready in case you need to put out the flame. Pour the Cointreau and brandy over the sauce without stirring. Immediately light the sauce with a match, standing well back from the pan. Serve the crêpes on warmed plates. Fresh vanilla ice cream is a lovely accompaniment.

Chef's tip Leftover crêpes can be stacked, wrapped in foil and frozen in an airtight bag. To defrost, refrigerate them overnight, then peel off to use. They are a handy and very versatile stand-by.

Burgundy granita

A granita in Italian—or granité in French—is a close cousin to the true sorbet. It is made with sharp-tasting fruit, spiked with wine or champagne. Due to its low sugar content, small crystals form during freezing, giving the dessert its name: a granita should always give the impression of crushed ice.

Preparation time **10 minutes + 3 hours freezing**
Total cooking time **5 minutes**
Serves 8

175 g (5³/4 oz) caster sugar
80 ml (2³/4 fl oz) orange juice
2 tablespoons lime juice
1 tablespoon chopped lemon balm or mint
750 ml (24 fl oz) Burgundy or other red wine
sprigs of lemon balm or mint, to garnish

1 Chill eight serving glasses in the refrigerator. Place the sugar, orange juice, lime juice, lemon balm or mint and 130 ml (4¹/4 fl oz) water in a pan over medium heat. Ensuring the mixture doesn't boil, stir until the sugar has dissolved. Bring to the boil, reduce the heat and simmer for 2–3 minutes.
2 Strain the syrup through a fine wire sieve, allow it to cool thoroughly, then add the wine. Stir well and pour the mixture into a shallow, freezer-proof container. Freeze for 3 hours, or until set.
3 When it is fully frozen and crystallised, scrape the granita into the chilled glasses using a metal spoon. Decorate each glass with sprigs of lemon balm or mint and serve at once.

Oeufs à la neige

*In English, this amazing dessert is better known as 'floating islands', or more literally
'snow eggs'. A rich custard sauce (crème anglaise) is topped with meltingly soft
meringues and drizzled with caramel sauce.*

Preparation time **40 minutes**
Total cooking time **40 minutes**
Serves **6–8**

SYRUP
185 g (6 oz) sugar

CREME ANGLAISE
500 ml (16 fl oz) milk
1 vanilla pod
6 egg yolks
125 g (4 oz) caster sugar

MERINGUES
6 egg whites
125 g (4 oz) caster sugar

CARAMEL SAUCE
100 g (3 1/4 oz) sugar
lemon juice, to taste

1 To make the syrup, dissolve the sugar in 2 litres water over low heat. Bring to the boil, then reduce the heat and leave to simmer gently.

2 To make the crème anglaise, prepare a large bowl of ice or iced water and place a smaller bowl inside. Place the milk and vanilla pod in a heavy-based pan, and just bring to the boil. Make the custard following the Chef's techniques on page 63, then strain into the prepared bowl in the ice. Leave to cool, stirring occasionally.

3 To make the meringues, beat the egg whites in a clean, dry bowl until stiff peaks form. Add the sugar and beat until smooth and glossy. Shape into 'eggs' using two large spoons dipped in water, then poach in the gently simmering syrup for 3 minutes, taking care not to crowd the pan. Turn using a slotted spoon and poach for 3 more minutes. Drain on a tea towel, and leave to cool.

4 To make the caramel sauce, place the sugar, 50 ml (1 3/4 fl oz) water and a few drops of lemon juice in a heavy-based saucepan. Stir over low heat until the sugar dissolves. Simmer for about 4–5 minutes, or until the caramel just takes on a golden colour: the sauce should be thick and syrupy. Stop the cooking immediately by plunging the saucepan into a large, heatproof bowl of iced water for a few seconds. Remove the saucepan and keep the caramel warm or it will harden.

5 To serve, fill a shallow bowl with crème anglaise and top with poached meringues. Drizzle the caramel over and serve the remaining sauce in a sauce boat.

Baked apple and fruit charlotte

*As legend has it, this famous moulded dessert was named after the wife of George III,
England's famous 'mad' king. It is traditionally set in a tall, bucket-shaped mould.*

Preparation time **30 minutes + 1 hour cooling**
Total cooking time **1 hour 20 minutes**
Serves 6

14 thin slices of white bread, trimmed of crusts
175 g (5¾ oz) unsalted butter
**500 g (1 lb) Granny Smith apples, peeled, cored and
finely chopped**
**500 g (1 lb) cooking apples, peeled, cored and finely
chopped**
90 g (3 oz) soft brown sugar
pinch of ground cinnamon
½ teaspoon ground nutmeg
50 g (1¾ oz) walnuts, finely chopped
50 g (1¾ oz) sultanas or other dried fruits
2 tablespoons marmalade (optional)
grated lemon rind (optional)
3 tablespoons apricot jam (see Chef's tips)

1 Brush a 1.25 litre charlotte mould with softened
butter. Cut six slices of bread in half to form rectangles;
cut five slices in half at a diagonal to form triangles.
Reserve the remaining three slices of bread.

2 Turn the mould upside down and place the bread
triangles on top, overlapping the edges to completely
cover the top of the mould. Hold the triangles in place
and, using the mould as a guide, trim the excess edges
with scissors so the triangles will fit inside the base of
the mould exactly.

3 Melt 150 g (5 oz) of the butter, dip the trimmed
triangles in, then line the base of the mould. Dip the
rectangles in butter and arrange around the sides,
overlapping the edges until the mould is completely
covered, filling any gaps with the bread trimmings. Dip
the reserved slices of bread in the butter and set aside.

4 To make the filling, melt the remaining butter in a
large pan. Add the apples, cover the pan with baking
paper and then a lid. Cook the apples over low heat
for 15–20 minutes, or until they are soft and of the
consistency of apple sauce. Add the sugar and stir over
high heat for about 5 minutes, or until the mixture falls
from the side of the spoon in wide drops. Stir in the
cinnamon, nutmeg, walnuts and sultanas. Remove from
the heat. Add the marmalade, and perhaps a little grated
lemon rind. Set aside to cool.

5 Preheat the oven to moderately hot 190°C (375°F/
Gas 5). Ladle the filling into the mould until half full.
Cover the filling with half the reserved bread slices,
press down firmly, then add the remaining filling. If the
filling is not level with the mould lining, trim the bread
carefully with the tip of a small knife or scissors. Cover
with the remaining reserved bread, taking care to fill any
gaps. Press in gently and cover with foil.

6 Place the charlotte on a baking tray and bake for
45 minutes to 1 hour, or until golden and firm. Leave to
cool completely before turning out onto a serving plate:
this should take about 1 hour.

7 Warm the apricot jam and 25 ml (¾ fl oz) water in a
small pan over low heat until melted. Brush the mixture
over the surface of the charlotte to give a light glaze.

Chef's tips A heatproof soufflé dish or cake tin can be
used instead of a charlotte mould.

   If the jam is very fruity, it will be easier to brush onto
the charlotte if it has been strained after warming. An
inexpensive jam is fine for this purpose.

   For extra zest, replace the sultanas with 1–2 tablespoons
chopped glacé ginger and the nutmeg with ground ginger.

   For an indulgent accompaniment, whip 150 ml
(5 fl oz) whipping cream with 50 g (1¾ oz) sugar, then
stir in 2 tablespoons of Calvados.

Gooseberry fool

England is the home of this old-fashioned but delicious dessert made of cooked, strained and puréed fruit, chilled and folded into custard and whipped cream. Traditionally, fool is made from gooseberries, although any fruit may be used.

*Preparation time **40 minutes + 2 hours refrigeration***
*Total cooking time **25 minutes***
*Serves **4–6***

GOOSEBERRY PUREE
120 g (4 oz) caster sugar
500 g (1 lb) fresh gooseberries, topped and tailed
1 leaf gelatine or 1/2 teaspoon gelatine powder

1 1/2 tablespoons cornflour
3 tablespoons caster sugar
125 ml (4 fl oz) milk
125 ml (4 fl oz) Greek or plain thick yoghurt
75 ml (2 1/2 fl oz) cream, for whipping
1 egg white
100 ml (3 1/4 fl oz) cream for whipping, to serve
4–6 macaroon biscuits, to serve

1 To make the purée, reserve 1 tablespoon of sugar and place the rest in a heavy-based pan with 250 ml (8 fl oz) water. Stir over low heat until the sugar dissolves. Bring to the boil, add the fruit, reduce the heat and simmer for 10 minutes, or until tender. Strain the liquid. Purée the fruit in a food processor, then stir in the reserved sugar.

2 Soak the gelatine leaf or powder, following the Chef's techniques on page 63.

3 In a separate heatproof bowl, combine the cornflour and 1 tablespoon of the sugar. Add 50 ml (1 3/4 fl oz) of the milk and stir until smooth. Bring the remaining milk almost to the boil, then whisk it into the cornflour and sugar. Place in a clean pan and whisk over low heat until the mixture boils and thickens. Remove from the heat.

4 Stir the soaked gelatine into the hot custard until dissolved, then cover with baking paper and leave to cool. Stir in the fruit purée and yoghurt, mixing well.

5 Whip the cream until soft peaks form, then fold into the custard. Whisk the egg white in a clean, dry bowl until stiff, then whisk in the remaining sugar and fold into the custard. Pipe or spoon the fool into tall glasses, ensuring there are no air pockets. Chill for 2 hours to set. Serve with freshly whipped cream and macaroons.

Chef's tip If the gooseberries are tart, sweeten them with a little sugar. Frozen gooseberries may be used in this recipe if fresh ones are not available.

Cabinet puddings

In this classic English dessert, leftover sponge cake is transformed into a scrumptious treat, often soaked in liqueur, dressed with dried fruit and custard, then baked in individual flower-pot shaped moulds. Cabinet pudding is usually served with fresh vanilla custard.

Preparation time **35 minutes**
Total cooking time **1 hour 20 minutes**
Serves 4

caster sugar, for dusting
100 g (3¹/4 oz) sponge cake
1 tablespoon glacé cherries, chopped
2 tablespoons currants
3 tablespoons sultanas
3 teaspoons Kirsch
2 eggs
1¹/2 tablespoons caster sugar
¹/2 teaspoon vanilla extract or essence
250 ml (8 fl oz) milk

1 Preheat the oven to slow 150°C (300°F/Gas 2). Lightly brush four 160 ml (5¹/4 fl oz) dariole moulds or ramekins with softened butter. Place some sugar in a mould and, without placing your fingers inside the mould, rotate it so that a layer of sugar adheres to the butter. Tap out any excess sugar and repeat with the other moulds.

2 Cut the sponge cake into 5 mm (¹/4 inch) cubes and mix in a bowl with the glacé cherries, currants and sultanas. Pour the Kirsch over, toss lightly, then leave to soak for a few minutes. Divide the cake and fruit mixture between the four moulds.

3 Beat the eggs lightly in a large heatproof bowl and whisk in the sugar and vanilla extract or essence. Warm the milk in a small, heavy-based pan until bubbles show around the edge of the pan. Follow the method for making custard in the Chef's techniques on page 63, then pour the custard into each of the moulds.

4 Half fill a baking dish or deep ovenproof dish with hot water, place the moulds inside and set aside for 5 minutes. Bake for 1 hour, or until the puddings are just firm to the light touch of a finger. Remove from the oven and cool for 3–4 minutes before turning out onto a warm serving dish. Serve with vanilla custard.

Gratin of fruits

Gratins are grilled until golden, giving a glorious, appetising colour. Here, a warm, rich sabayon provides a sensational topping to a simple medley of fresh fruit.

*Preparation time **30 minutes***
*Total cooking time **25–30 minutes***
Serves 4

2 peaches
2 nectarines
2 plums
4 lychees
2 passion fruit
250 g (8 oz) strawberries
250 g (8 oz) raspberries
2 eggs, plus 2 egg yolks
80 g (2³/4 oz) caster sugar
3 teaspoons Kirsch
fresh mint leaves, to decorate

1 Wash the peaches, nectarines and plums and dry them well. Cut the fruits in half, then twist the two halves in opposite directions to separate them. Remove the stones and thinly slice the fruits.

2 Peel away the tough brittle skin of the lychees. Slit each fruit down one side through to the stone, then open the flesh and remove the stone. Cut the passion fruit in half, scooping the pulp and seeds into a bowl. Rinse the strawberries and pull out the stalks. Arrange all the fruit decoratively on four heatproof plates or individual shallow dishes, then spoon the passion fruit pulp and seeds over the top.

3 Heat the grill to a high setting. Fill a pan with enough water so that the bottom of the bowl used in the next step does not touch the simmering water when placed over it. Bring the water to the boil, then reduce the heat to a simmer.

4 Place the eggs, yolks and sugar in a large heatproof bowl, then place the bowl over the pan of simmering water. Whisk for 10–15 minutes, or until the mixture becomes thick and creamy and leaves a trail as it falls from the whisk. Stir in the Kirsch.

5 Spoon the sauce over the fruit and grill quickly until the sabayon is an even brown. Decorate with mint leaves and serve.

Chef's tip The fruit plates can be prepared beforehand and covered with plastic wrap to prevent the fruit drying out.

Apple fritters

The apples in this classic favourite can be replaced with almost any fruit that cooks well. Bananas, pineapple and pears are perfect substitutes.

Preparation time **35 minutes**
Total cooking time **20 minutes**
Serves **6–8**

900 g (1 lb 13 oz) Golden Delicious apples
140 g (4¹/₂ oz) caster sugar
100 ml (3¹/₄ fl oz) Calvados
300 g (10 oz) plain flour
2 tablespoons potato starch or cornflour
2 eggs, plus 4 egg whites
250 ml (8 fl oz) beer
oil, for deep-frying
50 g (1³/₄ oz) icing sugar, to dust

1 Peel and core the apples, then slice them into 1 cm (1/2 inch) rounds so that each has a hole in the centre. Combine 100 g (3¹/₄ oz) of the sugar with the Calvados and use it to coat the apple. Set aside.

2 Sift the flour, starch and a pinch of salt into a large bowl. Make a well in the centre and whisk in the two eggs, the beer and then 1 tablespoon oil. Mix to a smooth, lump-free batter and set aside to rest. (The batter will be very thick, to coat and cook the apples.) Fill a large deep pan or deep fryer one third full of oil. Preheat to 170°C (325°F).

3 Beat the egg whites until soft peaks form, then add the remaining sugar. Beat until smooth and glossy. Fold into the batter with a large metal spoon.

4 Drain the apples on paper towels. Dip the slices in batter one at a time and deep-fry. Once browned, turn and cook the other side. Remove and drain on paper towels. Serve warm or hot, sprinkled with icing sugar.

Crêpes soufflées

An old French custom when cooking crêpes is to make a wish while flipping the crêpe, holding a coin in the hand for prosperity. Your guests will feel blessed indeed when offered this ambrosial dessert.

Preparation time **40 minutes + 1 hour resting**
Total cooking time **15 minutes**
Makes 9 crêpes

CREPE BATTER
2 tablespoons sugar
75 g (2¹/₂ oz) plain flour
I egg, lightly beaten
200 ml (6¹/₂ fl oz) milk
¹/₄ teaspoon vanilla extract or essence

unsalted butter, for cooking

SOUFFLE FILLING
225 ml (7¹/₄ fl oz) milk
¹/₄ vanilla pod, split lengthways
125 g (4 oz) sugar
4 egg yolks
2 tablespoons cornflour
I–2 teaspoons Grand Marnier
5 egg whites

1 To make the crêpes, sift the sugar, flour and a pinch of salt into a bowl. Make a well in the centre and add the egg. Whisk briskly to draw in the flour, slowly adding half the milk in a thin steady stream. Whisk until smooth. Add the vanilla and remaining milk, whisking constantly into a smooth batter—you may need to sieve the batter to remove all the lumps. Cover with plastic wrap and rest for at least 1 hour, preferably overnight.
2 Over medium heat, melt some butter in a 16–18 cm (6¹/₂–7 inch) heavy-based or non-stick pan; pour out any excess butter. Stir the batter well and pour into the pan from a ladle or jug, starting in the centre and swirling

the pan to create a thin coating. Cook for 1 minute, or until bubbles appear, the batter sets and the edges are brown. Carefully loosen and lift the edges with a palette knife or spatula. Turn and cook for 30 seconds, or until lightly golden. Remove from the pan with the first-fried side facing down. Set aside. Repeat with the remaining batter. When cooled, lightly sprinkle the crêpes with sugar and stack them, separated with greaseproof paper. Preheat the oven to moderate 180°C (350°F/Gas 4).
3 To make the soufflé filling, slowly bring the milk and vanilla pod to the boil in a medium pan. Remove from the heat and set aside for 3 minutes to infuse the milk. In a separate bowl, vigorously beat the sugar and egg yolks with a wire whisk until pale. Stir in the cornflour, gradually pour in the scalded milk and return the mixture to the pan. Stir for 2–3 minutes over moderate heat, or until thickened. Stir in the Grand Marnier, cover with baking paper and set aside to cool.
4 Remove the vanilla pod from the custard. In a separate bowl, whisk the egg whites until stiff peaks form. Using a large metal spoon, fold the egg whites into the custard in at least three batches. Gently fold until the mixture is well combined: it should be light and airy.
5 Place some filling on one half of the paler side of the crêpes. Fold over into a semicircle, but do not seal the edges. Place on a lightly greased oven tray and bake for 10–15 minutes. The crêpes will open slightly. Using a wide spatula, carefully place each crêpe onto a warm serving plate. The crêpes may be served with a chocolate or fruit sauce, but are also delicious on their own.

Chef's tip If the first crêpes stick, the pan may not be hot enough. Always present crêpes with the first-cooked side facing outwards: it is more nicely browned with a lovely lace-like pattern.

Chef's techniques

◆

Clarifying butter

Removing the water and solids from butter makes it less likely to burn. Ghee is a form of clarified butter.

To make 100 g (3¼ oz) clarified butter, cut 180 g (5¾ oz) butter into small cubes. Place in a small pan set into a larger pot of water over low heat. Melt the butter without stirring.

Remove the pan from the heat and allow to cool slightly. Skim the foam from the surface, being careful not to stir the butter.

Pour off the clear yellow liquid, being very careful to leave the milky sediment behind in the pan. Discard the sediment and store the clarified butter in an airtight container in the refrigerator.

Baking blind

Baking the pastry before adding the filling prevents the base becoming soggy during cooking.

After the pastry has been eased into the prepared tin, use a small ball of excess pastry to gently press the pastry into the sides of the tin around the fluted edges.

Use a rolling pin to trim the pastry edges. Gently but firmly roll across the top of the tin. Refrigerate for 10 minutes.

Prick the pastry shell to allow steam to escape during baking. Line with crumpled greaseproof or baking paper, fill with rice or baking beans and bake for the time specified in the recipe.

Remove the paper and the hot rice or baking beans. Discard the paper. The rice or beans can be stored and used over and over again after cooking.

Making custard

Slow cooking and gentle heat are required to prevent the custard curdling.

Whisk the hot, infused milk or cream into the beaten eggs and sugar. Pour into a clean pan.

Stir gently over low heat with a wooden spoon for 10–15 minutes, or until the custard coats the back of the spoon and leaves a clear parting when a finger is drawn across. Do not boil, or the eggs will scramble.

Strain the warm custard through a fine sieve into a clean jug to remove any lumps.

Making a soufflé ridge

A successful soufflé has a high 'cap' in the centre, just like a traditional chef's cap.

Run your thumb around the inside of the soufflé dish. The ridge this creates will help the soufflé rise evenly.

Making Italian meringue

Close-textured and shiny, this meringue holds up well for up to two days without cooking.

Boil without stirring until the syrup reaches the soft-ball stage, 116–118°C (241–244°F). If you do not have a sugar thermometer, drop 1/4 teaspoon of the syrup into iced water: it should hold its shape but be soft when pressed.

In a large heatproof bowl, beat the egg whites into soft peaks, using a balloon whisk or electric beaters. Avoiding the whisk, add the hot syrup in a thin steady stream, beating constantly until thick and glossy. Beat until cold.

Using gelatine

Leaf gelatine has no flavour or colour, gives a softer set than gelatine powder, and is easier to use.

Lower the leaves or sheets of gelatine into a bowl of cold water, adding each leaf separately to prevent sticking. Leave to soak for a few minutes, or until softened.

When the leaf is soft and pliable, carefully remove it and squeeze out any excess liquid. If you are using gelatine powder, dissolve each teaspoon of gelatine in 1 tablespoon of water, following the manufacturer's instructions.

Published by Murdoch Books® a division of Murdoch Magazines Pty Limited, 213 Miller Street, North Sydney NSW 2060.

Murdoch Books and Le Cordon Bleu thank the 32 masterchefs of all the Le Cordon Bleu Schools, whose knowledge and expertise have made this book possible, especially: Chef Cliche (MOF), Chef Terrien, Chef Boucheret, Chef Duchêne (MOF), Chef Guillut, Chef Steneck, Paris; Chef Males, Chef Walsh, Chef Hardy, London; Chef Chantefort, Chef Bertin, Chef Jambert, Chef Honda, Tokyo; Chef Salembien, Chef Boutin, Chef Harris, Sydney; Chef Lawes, Adelaide; Chef Guiet, Chef Denis, Ottawa. Of the many students who helped the Chefs test each recipe, a special mention to graduates David Welch and Allen Wertheim. A very special acknowledgment to Directors Susan Eckstein, Great Britain, and Kathy Shaw, Paris, who have been responsible for the coordination of the Le Cordon Bleu team throughout this series.

Murdoch Books®
Managing Editor: Kay Halsey
Series Concept, Design and Art Direction: Juliet Cohen
Editors: Katri Hilden, Alison Moss
Food Director: Jody Vassallo
Food Editors: Lulu Grimes, Kerrie Ray, Tracy Rutherford
Designer: Michèle Lichtenberger
Photographer: Chris Jones
Food Stylist: Mary Harris
Food Preparation: Kerrie Ray
Chef's Techniques Photographer: Reg Morrison
Home Economists: Joanna Beaumont, Michelle Earl, Michelle Lawton, Toiva Longhurst, Kerrie Mullins, Kerrie Ray

CEO & Publisher: Anne Wilson
Publishing Director: Catie Ziller
General Manager: Mark Smith
Creative Director: Marylouise Brammer
International Sales Director: Mark Newman

National Library of Australia Cataloguing-in-Publication Data
Desserts. ISBN 0 86411 736 1. 1. Desserts. (Series: Le Cordon Bleu home collection). 641.813

Printed by Toppan Printing (S) Pte Ltd
First Printed 1997
©Design and photography Murdoch Books® 1997
©Text Le Cordon Bleu 1997
Distributed in the UK by D Services, 6 Euston Street, Freemen's Common, Leicester LE2 7SS Tel 0116-254-7671 Fax 0116-254-4670. Distributed in Canada by Whitecap (Vancouver) Ltd, 351 Lynn Avenue, North Vancouver, BC V7J 2C4 Tel 604-980-9852 Fax 604-980-8197 or Whitecap (Ontario) Ltd, 47 Coldwater Road, North York, ON M3B 1Y8 Tel 416-444-3442 Fax 416-444-6630

The Publisher and Le Cordon Bleu wish to thank Carole Sweetnam for her help with this series.
Front cover: Thin shortbreads with fresh cream and fruit.

IMPORTANT INFORMATION

CONVERSION GUIDE

1 cup = 250 ml (8 fl oz)
1 Australian tablespoon = 20 ml (4 teaspoons)
1 UK tablespoon = 15 ml (3 teaspoons)

NOTE: We have used 20 ml tablespoons. If you are using a 15 ml tablespoon, for most recipes the difference will be negligible. For recipes using baking powder, gelatine, bicarbonate of soda and flour, add an extra teaspoon for each tablespoon specified.

CUP CONVERSIONS—DRY INGREDIENTS

1 cup flour, plain or self-raising = 125 g (4 oz)
1 cup sugar, caster = 250 g (8 oz)
1 cup breadcrumbs, dry = 125 g (4 oz)

IMPORTANT: Those who might be at risk from the effects of salmonella food poisoning (the elderly, pregnant women, young children and those suffering from immune deficiency diseases) should consult their GP with any concerns about eating raw eggs.